DRIVING
TEST TIPS

Summersdale Publishers Ltd
46 West Street
Chichester
West Sussex
PO19 1RP
UK

www.summersdale.com

Printed and bound in Great Britain

ISBN 1 84024 389 9

CONTENTS

Introduction.............................5

The theory test..........................6

Before the test day.....................11

Banish those nerves!...................30

The day of the test....................47

What to wear...........................60

Driving tips............................65

Why people fail........................91

If you fail.............................121

INTRODUCTION

This book won't teach you to drive, but if you think you know how to drive and are worried about the test then this is what you need to overcome that anxiety. You could have all the knowledge and driving skills necessary to pass your test but if nerves cause you to make a silly mistake it can all be wasted. Passing your driving test is as much about learning to take control of yourself as it is about taking control of your vehicle. It sounds a tall order but it's really very simple. Just follow the tips in this book, try to relax and give it your best shot…

The theory test

OVERVIEW

It is now necessary to pass a driving theory test before being allowed to take the practical test. This theory test replaces the questions examiners used to ask their candidates at the end of the drive. Its implementation has improved the safety of examiners by eliminating the need for them to go out on the road with candidates who do not understand essential road signs and rules. It also aims to improve general road safety by raising the standards of all new drivers.

Test yourself   (answers on p. 127)

MULTIPLE CHOICE SECTION

The first part of the theory test consists of 35 multiple choice questions covering a wide range of topics concerning driving rules, signs, safety and aspects of *The Highway Code*. You have 40 minutes to answer 30 or more questions correctly. Study *The Highway Code* and do as many mock theory tests as you can.

MOCK THEORY TESTS

Visit www.dsa.gov.uk where you can do
a full mock multiple choice theory test on
the Internet. You can also buy various
CD-ROMs for your computer containing
several practice tests.

Test yourself   (answers on p. 127)

HAZARD AWARENESS SECTION

The second part of the theory test is an electronic test of your awareness of potential hazards on the road using interactive video clips. You have approximately 15 minutes to obtain a minimum score of 44 out of a possible 75. The minimum pass rate is higher for those taking lorry or bus tests.

Before the test day

DON'T RUSH THINGS

Only book your test when you and your instructor think you're ready. If you take a test too soon you're going to feel the extra stress that comes from knowing you're not fully prepared.

MAKE THE DECISION

The driving test itself is not where you pass or fail. By then, in many ways, it's too late. The work needed to pass gets done before the test and it's up to you to show the examiner that you've done that work and deserve to pass.

Test yourself  (answers on p. 127)

PLAN AHEAD

Your driving test is a major landmark in your life. It's important to focus on it, so avoid booking a test that might coincide with other major life events such as exams, new babies, house moves, weddings, etc.

BE FAMILIAR WITH YOUR CAR

All makes of car feel slightly different to drive, so don't change cars just before the test. The indicator lever might be on the other side of the steering wheel; the brakes might require more effort than you're used to; the switch for the lights might be somewhere different; the turning circle might be larger. It's important to be confident with your car and sticking with the same car is the only way to do that.

Test yourself (answers on p. 127)

DO A COUPLE OF MOCK TESTS

Your instructor will be able to take you
through one or two mock tests,
preferably starting and finishing at the site
of the driving test centre. That way when
it comes to the real thing you'll already
know what it feels like to drive out of
that car park and onto the road.
You can also practise for the written
exam with help from friends and
family testing you on the questions.

DO A MOCK DRIVING TEST IMMEDIATELY BEFORE THE REAL ONE

Your driving instructor should take you round 'the course' just before you do the real test so that the area feels familiar and you're fully in tune with your car and the roads.

Test yourself   (answers on p. 127)

PRACTISE IN ALL WEATHERS

An emergency stop on a dry road is very different to one in heavy rain. Since you won't be able to predict the weather on your test day make sure you're comfortable about driving in all weather conditions. An understanding of skid control will help if you have to stop suddenly in the wet.

BOOK A MORNING
TEST IF POSSIBLE

Mid morning is best, as it gives you time to feel awake. Morning test times are preferable to afternoon ones because they give you less time to feel worried.

Test yourself (answers on p. 127)

DON'T ANNOUNCE THE TEST DATE TO THE WORLD

If you feel pressured by having everyone giving you advice and recalling their own driving test nightmare experiences, then don't tell them. If you pass you'll have a great surprise for them.

TURN YOUR WEAKNESSES INTO STRENGTHS

Everyone has their weaknesses when it comes to driving lessons. It might be roundabouts, parking or changing gear smoothly. Don't overlook these problems: identify them and get your instructor to help you work at them until they become your strongest skills.

DON'T IGNORE ASPECTS OF DRIVING THAT YOU DON'T ENJOY

If you hate parallel parking, practise it until you can do it with your eyes closed. Don't get a mental block about aspects of driving that you hate – just do it.

CHECK OUT THE SAFETY OF THE TEST CAR

If you're going to take the test in your own car rather than your instructor's, make sure it has a second rear-view mirror for the examiner to use. Also make sure it's clean and tidy and that the passenger seat belt functions correctly; the examiner won't come out on the test with you if there's anything wrong with it.

Test yourself (answers on p. 127)

CHECK OUT THE LEGALITY OF THE TEST CAR

The tax disc, the insurance and the MOT must all be up to date. The speedometer must read in miles per hour. The examiner will refuse to go out in any car that isn't fully legal. Also check that your L-plates haven't fallen off and that they are clearly displayed.

UNDER THE BONNET

Part of the driving test includes testing
your knowledge of basic car maintenance.
You'll need to know how to check and
top up oil, coolant, brake fluid
and washer fluid.

Test yourself   (answers on p. 127)

TYRES

You need to know how to check
whether the tyres are at the correct
pressure and have sufficient tread, and
how to spot signs of damage that could
make them unsafe for driving.

LIGHTS

Learn how to check that all the car's lights are working, including brake lights and indicators.

BRAKES

A demonstration that the brakes are in working order may be required before driving off in the test. Make sure your instructor shows you how to do this, plus how to test and look for signs of wear in the handbrake.

OTHER CAR FEATURES

Whatever your car offers by way of
features, it's important to know how
to operate them and how to check if
they are not working. This includes the
horn and power steering but doesn't
apply to non-control items such as the
stereo. It can also include heaters and
de-misters and you'll be expected to
use them if appropriate.

Test yourself (answers on p. 127)

Banish those nerves!

UNDERSTAND NERVES

A state of nervousness is the body's evolved reaction to danger. It creates a change in a person's biochemical balance that enables a short-term enhancement of strength and senses designed to either get that person out of danger quickly by running, or to help them fight. Feeling nervous will help you provided you don't let your worries get out of control.

KEEP AN EYE ON STRESS

Don't ignore worries about your driving test. Stress can build up as multiple factors combine until you can't cope any more, so try to deal with every problem as it occurs so that the stress is always manageable. This also applies to stresses of everyday life – keep them under control and you'll find you can cope with your driving test too.

EAT THE RIGHT THINGS

A balanced diet of natural and healthy foods will help your body to cope with stress more easily. Too much sugar or caffeine will exacerbate any feelings of stress you may have.

BUT ALSO EAT CHOCOLATE

Despite chocolate's high sugar content there are other ingredients that are known to have a calming effect.

DON'T CHANGE YOUR DIET AT THE LAST MINUTE

Suddenly switching to a new kind of diet, such as carbohydrate-free, just a few days before the driving test can unnecessarily complicate your body's ability to cope with stress.

Test yourself (answers on p. 127)

GO TO BED

Make time to relax and feel tired the night before the test. If you can get a good night's sleep your concentration levels will be improved.

WIND DOWN AT NIGHT

If the looming test day leaves you
anxious last thing at night try to wind
down with a hot bath or some
soothing music.

Test yourself (answers on p. 127)

BE PREPARED FOR BROKEN SLEEP

If you can't sleep well then don't fight it. Getting worked up about a sleepless night only makes it harder to sleep and leaves you more exhausted the next morning. It's normal to have broken sleep patterns when a scary driving test approaches, so plan for this and try to find ways to minimise light and noise pollution in your bedroom to help you sleep. Drinking warm milk may help, too, as it is said that this reduces gastric secretion, influences stomach receptors and has a sedative effect.

DON'T CHEAT YOUR BODY

You might think pills are a good way to calm the nerves, but they can impair concentration and slow your reaction times. Drinking heavily the night before the test in order to relax will also not help the next day. What's more, you could still have alcohol in your system when you come to take the test. Your body needs to be fresh and alert, not drugged-up and dazed.

Test yourself  (answers on p. 127)

AVOID SMOKING

Some people smoke to alleviate stress, but it also increases blood pressure and can add to feelings of anxiety.

BREATHE

If the looming test date causes anxiety,
try breathing techniques. It's simple:
breathe in deep, hold for a second,
breathe out. Repeat several times, and
focus on nothing but your breathing.
It helps to empty your mind of worries
and calms your heart rate.

Test yourself (answers on p. 127)

BELIEVE IN YOURSELF

You can do it. You've worked hard for this. You know how to drive. Think of a couple of particularly good lessons you've had recently, and take pleasure in the thought of showing off your skills to a sceptical examiner.

REMIND YOURSELF THAT YOU HAVE PASSED OTHER EXAMS IN YOUR LIFE

A driving test is an exam like any other. You've taken and passed exams that are much tougher than the driving test – don't forget that.

Test yourself (answers on p. 127)

REMEMBER, THE EXAMINER IS HUMAN

They understand that you're nervous. They know the test means a lot to you. Within reason they will make allowances for this, especially in the first minute or so, provided your nervousness doesn't compromise safety.

MEDITATE

Find five minutes each day in the week before the test to sit in a quiet place, close your eyes, and let your mind take you to a beach where the waves are lapping at your toes and the sun is warming your body. This will help to prevent a build-up of pre-test nerves.

RELAX YOUR MUSCLES

Muscle tension caused by stress can
be alleviated by exercise and by the
simple technique of tensing your whole
body and then relaxing the muscles
and feeling the stress flowing
out of you as you do so.

The day of the test

TAKE A SHOWER

Make yourself clean and presentable
so the examiner won't pre-judge
you with any negative opinions.

EAT SOMETHING

You might feel too nervous to eat a good
breakfast, but getting some food inside
you will help your concentration.

RELY ON SLEEP, NOT CAFFEINE

Many candidates take energy drinks and tablets to compensate for lack of sleep. But high caffeine doses won't give you the same mental awareness as a good night's sleep. *The Highway Code* recommends two cups of coffee to combat tiredness, but no amount of artificial stimulation is as good as getting the sleep you need in the first place.

HAVE A POSITIVE ATTITUDE

Start the day with a positive mental approach, telling yourself this is going to be the day that you pass your driving test and looking forward to the celebrations that night.

REHEARSE IN YOUR HEAD

Take a moment to sit and go through some likely scenarios in your head. Picture yourself driving smoothly and confidently. Imagine feeling relaxed and listening attentively to the examiner's instructions whilst remaining focused on the road ahead and the vehicles around you.

THINK AHEAD

One day you'll be an experienced driver.
You'll drive every day without giving it a
second thought. You'll be tuning the
radio, checking your hair in the mirror,
talking on your hands-free phone and
assuming all the other bad habits that
most people have whilst driving along.
Try to picture yourself driving with
that much confidence and take that
confidence with you into the test.

Test yourself  (answers on p. 127)

RELISH THE NERVES

Being a little nervous puts your body in
a slightly hyper state, fuelled by adrenalin
that heightens your concentration
and performance. Don't be scared
of the feeling – harness it and
use it to your advantage.

RATIONALISE

It's not rocket science: millions of people have already passed the test you are about to take. It was important to every one of them, just like it is to you, but they all managed to get through it so it can't be that hard.

VISUALISE SUCCESS

Experiments have shown that students who visualise themselves succeeding are more likely to succeed than those who don't, and yet most students spend their time pessimistically visualising failure.

WEAR A WATCH

You don't want to be late for the test.
There's no flexibility – if you miss your
slot you'll have to book and pay for
another test. Make sure you arrive
at the test centre early.

REMEMBER THE DOCUMENTS

You'll need various documents in order
to be able to take the test: theory pass
certificate, provisional licence, identification,
etc. Your instructor will confirm the
current legal requirements.

CHECK THE SEAT POSITION

Make sure the seat is in the right position
for you to operate the controls
comfortably and that the mirrors
are correctly set.

What to wear

CHOOSE COMFORT OVER STYLE

No examiner will pass you because you have good dress sense. Dress for comfort and practicality rather than fashion.

SELECT THE RIGHT SHOES

Flat shoes or low-heeled shoes tend to be more practical for driving. If your shoes are so broad that it's hard to hit the brake pedal without hitting one of the other pedals at the same time, or if your stilettos don't give you the ankle leverage you need to depress the clutch fully, you're going to have problems. Lightweight trainers are usually the best option: the rubber soles give you a good grip on the pedals.

KEEP YOUR SHOES ON

Some people like to drive with no shoes
at all, enjoying the feel of the pedals on
bare feet. Although it's important to feel
the pedals, shoes give the extra power
to the feet that's needed in emergency
braking situations. It's hard to hit the
brake pedal for an emergency stop
with no shoes on because it hurts!

IF YOU NEED
GLASSES, WEAR THEM

If you need glasses to drive, make sure
they are in good condition and that you
wear them. If you fail the eyesight test
you won't even get to drive out
of the car park.

Driving tips

COME PREPARED

Before you drive off you will have to answer some elementary questions about vehicle safety and maintenance. Get them all wrong and you won't have the opportunity to show your driving skills – it's an automatic fail.

AIM FOR COMPETENCE NOT PERFECTION

The examiner is looking for a safe, competent driver. You don't have to be perfect. Small mistakes won't necessarily fail you so long as they don't represent a safety risk.

Test yourself (answers on p. 127)

LISTEN…

… to what your examiner is telling you to do. If you don't understand an instruction don't be afraid to ask for clarification. Did he mean to turn left or to take the left lane? Far better to ask than to guess wrong and end up with a fail.

EXPLAIN YOURSELF

If you find yourself in a situation where the road conditions are forcing you to do something contrary to the examiner's instructions, such as failing to get into the appropriate lane due to density of traffic, just explain what you're doing and why, and propose an alternative.

Test yourself   (answers on p. 127)

DON'T GIVE UP

If you think you've made a mistake that will result in failure, don't give up. Accept it, relax and keep driving until the test is over. It's always possible that the examiner either didn't notice the mistake or didn't plan to fail you because of it. Correct your own mistakes quickly. If you change to the wrong gear, fix it immediately. If you stall, enter the stall drill straight away without sighing or cursing.

RELAX, PASSING IS DOWN TO YOU

The examiner won't fail you just because he passed the previous two people. You will pass if you drive in a manner that demonstrates you're safe to be let loose on the roads. It's up to you to show that; convince the examiner by your competence and the driving license is in the bag.

Test yourself (answers on p. 127)

START IT RIGHT

Gearstick in neutral, handbrake on. Even
if you know they're in those positions,
demonstrate to the examiner that
you're checking.

KEEP IT SMOOTH

Part of demonstrating your competence in the car is to give a smooth ride for the examiner. This means smooth gear changes, the right speed around corners, braking progressively and in good time and not hitting anything!

Test yourself   (answers on p. 127)

KEEP IT REAL

Remind yourself as you drive that the examiner is not looking to recruit a racing driver or a police pursuit driver. Your only requirement is to drive normally, like everyone else on the road (or like they *should* be driving, anyway). You know how to drive normally, so just do it.

PACE YOURSELF

Don't be forced into sudden evasive manoeuvres by not thinking ahead. Your driving and your thinking should be at a steady pace – don't let your thinking lag behind or your driving race ahead of your ability to control it.

Test yourself (answers on p. 127)

PREPARE FOR THE UNEXPECTED

Anything could happen on the test and part of your job as driver is to demonstrate your ability to cope with real-world situations that arise. If you face a situation you've not encountered before, such as a police roadblock, try not to panic. Look at what the other cars around you are doing. Follow instructions from the police or your examiner. Take your time and understand the situation, and look at the options open to you before taking a decision.

REMEMBER, SILENCE MEANS GO STRAIGHT

If the examiner doesn't give you any instructions for a while, you should assume you're meant to keep going. Therefore at a crossroads or a mini-roundabout go straight over. Choose the appropriate lane for continuing on the same route when faced with a choice and no instructions.

Test yourself (answers on p. 127)

BE AWARE AT ROUNDABOUTS

Concentrate on the road signs as well as the instructions from the examiner. For some roundabouts the instruction 'take the second exit' requires you to be in the left lane, for others you might need to be in the right lane and on some you have a choice. Make sure you're aware of the position of your exit relative to your start position on the roundabout.

DON'T STOP UNNECESSARILY

At 'give way' junctions and roundabouts you don't have to stop moving. Slow down enough to be certain that the road is clear and to be able to negotiate the turn, but only stop completely if you have to wait for traffic to pass, if a traffic light or police officer tells you to do so or if it's an actual 'stop' junction.

Test yourself (answers on p. 127)

USE THE HANDBRAKE
APPROPRIATELY

Always use the handbrake if stopping on
a hill or for more than a couple of
seconds, but not indiscriminately at
every pause in the traffic.

TAKE THE NEXT AVAILABLE TURN

When instructed to turn into the next available road, make sure you're aware of any 'unavailable' roads that might come first, such as no entry roads. Your examiner expects you to have the common sense to take the next turn that is actually legal. If you feel the instruction is ambiguous because there's a small road coming up that you think might be a private drive or a car park entrance instead of a proper junction, just ask for clarification.

ANTICIPATE

Look out for signs of potential hazards ahead. Your examiner will be impressed if you anticipate a car about to pull out in front of you or a pedestrian about to cross the road. Observing people and cars ahead (both stationary and moving) is a matter of common sense. For instance, a smoky-looking exhaust from a parked car on a cold day is a sign that the engine's just been turned on and the driver is likely to be about to pull out; children playing football near the road could suddenly kick the ball into the street and run after it.

TAKE EXTRA CARE
MOVING TO THE RIGHT

It's always possible that someone may try
to overtake you, so a final check before
turning right or changing lanes to the
right is essential. This also applies when
changing lanes to the left – although no
one is meant to overtake you on the
inside that doesn't mean they won't try.
Even if the other car is breaking the law
you'll fail your test if you don't spot them
whizzing past you on the inside lane.

Test yourself   (answers on p. 127)

CONTROL THE CAR
WITH CONFIDENCE

Use the gears as they are intended.
Don't be afraid to change gear often.
If you stay in a low gear at high speed,
even for a short distance, it's a sign
of a nervous driver.

DRIVE AT THE RIGHT SPEED FOR THE ROAD

Speed limits vary all the time, so demonstrate to your examiner that you're aware of these different limits by speeding up where appropriate and safe to do so and slowing down before entering lower limit areas.

Test yourself (answers on p. 127)

KEEP YOUR EYE
ON THE ROAD

Most of your car's controls are designed
to be used without the driver having to
look at them. You should be able to use
the foot pedals, change gear and indicate
without taking an eye off the road.

DON'T SHOW OFF TOO MUCH

Proudly display your regular driving skills, but don't show off in the same way you might be tempted to give your friends a thrill when driving them. You may be confident that you can get the car through a tight gap between other vehicles, but if you charge through that gap so fast that you frighten the examiner it won't win you any favours.

Test yourself  (answers on p. 127)

DEMONSTRATE FULL AWARENESS OF THE ROAD

That means what's ahead of you and what's behind. Using mirrors correctly will show that you're aware of surrounding traffic – make sure you always use the rear-view mirror before applying the brakes, unless it's an emergency stop, and before you indicate.

MASTER THE REVERSE GEAR

Various manoeuvres will require the use of reverse gear – three-point turns, parallel parking and reversing around a corner are the most common. Try to look over your shoulder rather than just rely on the mirrors. Get in tune with how the steering wheel operates when going backwards and make sure you always stop if there's another car approaching.

Test yourself (answers on p. 127)

MASTER THE MANOEUVRES

Not knowing which manoeuvres you'll be asked to do nor feeling confident that you'll be able to do them can be the biggest causes of stress on the test day. Ask your instructor for clear rules or 'tricks' (for example, lining up the centre of the rear windscreen with the edge of the pavement when reversing round a corner).

Why people fail

JUNCTIONS

The most common reason people fail is because they don't know how to negotiate junctions. This covers roundabouts, traffic lights, crossroads and other junctions, and can involve failure to indicate correctly, taking the wrong lane and taking the turn in a less than safe and legal manner.

REVERSING
ROUND A CORNER

This is the second most common cause
of failure. It's a skill that takes practice and
development of spatial awareness.
Remember to ask your instructor for tips
and keep at it in your lessons until you
get it right every time.

Test yourself   (answers on p. 127)

STEERING

The third most common cause of test failure is incorrect steering. This includes the way you hold and turn the wheel and your skill at keeping the vehicle safely on the road and in its lane while cornering and turning.

PARKING

Fourth in the list of most common failure causes is parking. Practice is the only way to make sure your parking is good enough to pass.

Test yourself (answers on p. 127)

GEARS

The fifth most common cause of failure is incorrect use of the gears. Your choice of gear should be instinctive by the time you take the test. If you're still having to think about which gear is appropriate then you haven't done enough driving.

MIRRORS

Improper use of the mirror is next on the list of failure reasons. Usually it's due to not looking in the mirror when necessary, or looking during or after a manoeuvre instead of before. It can also be for failing to act on what is seen in the mirror; it's no use looking in the mirror if you don't take notice of what you see in it.

SPEED

Surprisingly, it's driving too slowly that fails more people than driving too fast. Don't drive like a nervous learner – drive like you know what you're doing and can cope in modern cut-throat busy roads.

TURNING RIGHT

This manoeuvre is the eighth most common cause of failure. You have to know the rules of the road instinctively and you have to have enough experience to be confident in applying those rules to the situation.

HESITANCY

If you pause too long when it's clearly safe to proceed at a junction then you're holding up traffic behind you and demonstrating that you're not yet a fully competent driver. Worse still, waiting too long to proceed sometimes means that you end up pulling out in front of approaching cars forcing them to slow down. It's the ninth most common cause of failure.

PULLING AWAY

Whether you're paused or parked, there are procedures for pulling away and joining the flow of traffic. Using an incorrect technique to do this is the tenth most common cause of failure.

EMERGENCY STOP

Skidding by braking too hard or failing to stop quickly enough by braking too softly won't convince the examiner that you can be relied upon to act safely if a child runs into the road.

STOPPING DISTANCE

If you let your concentration lapse and
end up too close to the car in front
then it's likely you'll fail.

ACCELERATOR

If used with a 'heavy right foot' then this pedal can fail you. Similarly, over-revving the engine through poor co-ordination with the clutch and generally displaying lack of competence will result in failure.

CLUTCH

Whether it's riding the clutch, inadequate
depression leading to a stalled engine
or a crunchy gear change, failure to
show control of this pedal can
mean failing the test.

FOOTBRAKE

Braking should be smooth and progressive, so that as your speed decreases the amount of pressure on the footbrake is reduced. This avoids sudden jolting stops. If the footbrake is used too late, too soon, too sharply or not at all, it can fail you.

HANDBRAKE

Usage before stopping, not releasing it before moving, not pulling it hard enough or not using it at all when you should can lead to failure. On hill starts, develop a sense of balance between the pull of the engine and the pull of the handbrake before releasing it.

STOP JUNCTIONS

These are different from normal 'give way' junctions for a reason: the view of the road is usually restricted and can only be observed once your vehicle is stationary. So make sure you stop completely before moving on even if the road is clear. Coasting towards the sign without stopping and then pulling straight onto the other road can be a cause of failure.

SIGNALS

The whole point of indicating is to help other road users anticipate your movements. If your signals are misleading, too soon, too late or missing entirely, then it's a fail. It's best to indicate even if you don't see any other vehicles around, because there might be other road users that you didn't spot (such as pedestrians) who will base their decision as to when to cross the road on your signals.

Test yourself (answers on p. 127)

NOT BEING READY

Some people take the test hoping for a fluke, knowing their driving skills are not consistently good enough to guarantee a pass. This usually results in failure.

EYESIGHT

Failure of the simple eyesight test is usually a result of forgetting to wear glasses or wearing glasses unsuited to driving.

Test yourself   (answers on p. 127)

OVERWHELMED BY STRESS

When stress can't be controlled it leads to panic. In that state of mind students perform very poorly. They can't think straight, can't concentrate, can't function. Often this happens to people who can drive well in their lessons but who cannot cope with the pressure of the real test. Use the techniques given earlier in this book to help you manage your stress levels.

OVERWHELMED
BY PRESSURE

Students often think more about the significance the test has to their future lives and careers than they do about the mechanics of actually passing it. If a driving licence is a crucial step towards your chosen career then the sense of pressure can make it harder to drive well. Again, refer to the stress-reducing techniques mentioned earlier.

Test yourself (answers on p. 127)

OVERCONFIDENCE

Eliminating all signs of test-related stress
is generally a good thing, but if it makes
you too confident of your skills or
in denial of the reality of your state
of preparedness then it can have
a negative effect. Balance your
confidence with respect for the
road and for the examiner.

DRIVING FAULTS (MINOR)

Not every error made in a driving test is enough on its own to warrant a fail. The examiner will classify the fault as a minor one if it doesn't represent a direct safety hazard (such as crunching the gears or stalling at a junction). But collect too many minor faults and you'll be failed anyway. Currently it takes 16 driving faults to fail.

PRE-ASSUMPTION OF FAILURE

Pessimistic students do themselves no favours by assuming they will fail before they have even arrived at the test centre. This negative attitude reduces the chances of success.

Test yourself (answers on p. 127)

SCARED EXAMINER

If the examiner thinks your driving style is
putting them in danger, they can stop the
test at any point and fail you on the spot.
This is done for their protection and for
that of other road users.

YOU'RE NOT READY TO
BANISH THOSE L-PLATES

You have to earn the right to remove
the L-plates, and the test is your chance
to demonstrate that you're ready. If you
can't prove it then the plates stay on

Test yourself No vehicles (answer

SERIOUS FAULTS

If a fault is judged to be serious, then the whole test will be failed. A serious fault is one that has the potential to be dangerous but doesn't involve a third party. Failing five 'show and tell' questions prior to the driving part of the test also constitutes a serious fault.

Test yourself (answers on p. 127)

DANGEROUS FAULTS

These are often instances when the examiner has to intervene to prevent an accident, either by giving you verbal instructions or trying to take control of the car. A dangerous fault means instant failure. If another road user has to swerve to avoid you, if you have an accident or if the examiner feels you have executed a dangerous manoeuvre then you will fail.

If you fail

FOCUS YOUR LESSONS

You will be told why you failed. Often it will be just one or two reasons. Sounds harsh? Maybe, but it means that the rest of your driving was good enough and all you need to do is focus your next few lessons on the weak areas that have been identified.

TAKE RESPONSIBILITY

An examiner wants you to demonstrate responsibility. A car is potentially dangerous and has to be driven responsibly. Think about whether you're really able to demonstrate adequate responsibility yet or whether you need to improve your vehicle control and knowledge.

IMPROVE YOUR CONFIDENCE

Don't take failure badly. You need to improve your confidence, not allow it to take a knock. Build up your confidence at driving before taking the test again.

KEEP YOUR EYES ON THE ROAD

If you failed because you're not demonstrating sufficient awareness of the traffic around you it could be because you're concentrating too much on what's happening inside your car when you drive. Changing gear, indicating, steering and braking should all be instinctive. Make sure you can drive without taking your eye off the road before booking a re-test.

Test yourself **STOP** (answers on p. 127)

CHECK YOUR ATTITUDE

If you failed because your attitude showed aggression or lack of consideration towards other road users, including pedestrians, you need to look at your whole approach to driving. Do you see every other vehicle as an annoyance getting in your way? Do you feel everyone is out to stop you getting from A to B quickly enough? If so, remember that the roads don't belong to you. You've got to share them with everyone else, fast or slow. Accept it, deal with it and relax.

ANSWERS

p. 7   pedestrian crossing
p. 9   tunnel ahead
p. 13   dual carriageway ends
p. 15   crossroads
p. 17   wild animals
p. 19   uneven road
p. 21   maximum speed (40 mph)
p. 23   no entry for vehicular traffic
p. 25   no U-turns
p. 27   no right turn
p. 29   no overtaking
p. 31   no cycling
p. 33   no stopping (clearway)
p. 35   loose chippings
p. 37   bend to right (or left if symbol reversed)
p. 39   road narrows on both sides
p. 41   opening or swing bridge ahead
p. 43   frail elderly people (or blind or disabled as shown) crossing road
p. 45   level crossing with barrier or gate ahead
p. 49   traffic queues likely ahead
p. 51   hump bridge
p. 53   traffic signals
p. 55   cattle
p. 57   slippery road
p. 59   no vehicles carrying explosives
p. 61   no towed caravans
p. 63   T-junction
p. 67   double bend first to left (symbol may be reversed)
p. 69   no buses (over 8 seats)
p. 71   area in which cameras are used to enforce traffic regulations
p. 73   no through road for vehicles
p. 75   quayside or river bank
p. 77   low-flying aircraft or sudden aircraft noise
p. 79   no vehicle or combination of vehicles over length shown
p. 81   give way to traffic on major road
p. 83   roundabout
p. 85   national speed limit applies
p. 87   two-way traffic crosses one-way road
p. 89   accompanied horse or ponies
p. 93   falling or fallen rocks
p. 95   road narrows on right (left if symbol reversed)
p. 97   worded warning sign
p. 99   no motor vehicles
p.101   road works
p.103   steep hill downwards
p.105   school crossing patrol
p.107   no vehicles over height shown
p.109   no vehicles over width shown
p.111   no goods vehicles over maximum gross weight shown (in tonnes) except for loading and unloading
p.113   no left turn
p.115   no waiting
p.117   no vehicles except bicycles being pushed
p.119   wild horses or ponies
p.123   risk of ice
p.125   stop and give way

De-stress for
EXAMS

summersdale *self-help*